Dr Jack's ILLUSTRATED SOUTH AFRICAN BYRD BOOK

DR JACK'S
ILLUSTRATED
SOUTH AFRICAN BYRD BOOK

or

THE MUTANT GUIDE TO SOUTH AFRICAN BYRDS
(with illustrations by Dr Jack)

Media House Publications

First published in 1990
Second Impression 1991
Third Impression 1991
Fourth Impression 1992
Fifth Impression 1993
Media House Publications
P.O. Box 782395 Sandton 2146 South Africa
Reg no 83/05894/07

ISBN 0 9583080 2 0

Concept: Dr Kate
Editorial: Dr Howard
Design: Dr Marthinus with illustration by Dr Jack
Title Input: Dr Malcolm
Index: Dr No

Printed in South Africa by Dr Creda

Title page: **Bearded Robin** *Erythropygia quadrivirgata*
Back cover: **Black Eagle** *Aquila verreauxii*

INTRODUCTION

BOOKS OF THIS NATURE and quality are as rare as cuckoo nests. We may be thankful for this, but it is not without awe that we welcome a brand new artiste to the wonderful world of ornithological illustrative interpretation. Hi, new bird artist!

Dr. Jack follows a long line of distinguished misinformants, but not since Anders Sparrman followed his *Honey-guide* in search of the legendary *Unicorn* has so much been revealed about so many species in a single volume. Or, to coin a phrase, never in a field-guide of flight has so much been borrowed by a non-medical doctor out of the blue.

We may wonder at the title the good Jack has bestowed upon himself. Could there be some secondary linkage to the famous apothecary, Heinrich Claudius? Probably not. But Heinie's *Namaqua Dove,* in its day (when bird books still included culinary suggestions – and there was no copyright, which incensed Simon van de Stel because it was his idea), was every bit as brilliant as Dr. Jack's *Scarce Swift.*

Birds in South Africa, prior to 1652, undoubtedly had African names, for example the onomatopoeic *mahem,* the *mossie* and even the *willie.* The Europeans that followed were driven, to some extent, by the hope that naming species after themselves would make them immortal, at least in the scientific world. How easy it must have been to bag a few specimens on the slopes of Table Mountain; measure, weigh, bundle up with the family name and despatch to the most convenient zoological headquarters! Certainly the species depicted in this volume have not been adequately described before and it is a tribute to the modesty of the artist that none bears his name. We can expect, however, some adjustment to the vernacular after Dr Jack's first sojourn into the field of bird re-identification.

Considering the number of birds shot in the name of scientific exploration and discovery, it is reasonable to assume that ornithologists have contributed to the decline of certain birds. In this, Dr Jack will have no part and he implores (with James Lovelock) all conventional scientists to "... come join me in independence, you have nothing to lose but your grants."

Happily, although there are more than 40 species included in this book, Dr Jack is confident that there are sufficient for a sequel. We look forward to *The Reluctant Mutant Guide...*

Drs Klip en Koke
Kew Gardens (near Alex) 1990

Pigmy Falcon *Polihierax semitorquatus*

Grassbird *Sphenoeacus afer*

Shy Albatross *Diomedia cauta*

Firecrowned Bishop *Euplectes hordeaceus*

Redfaced Mousebird *Colius indicus*

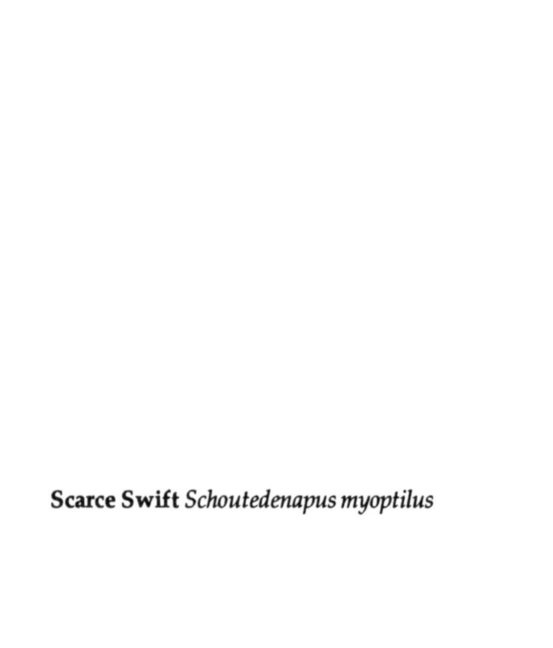

Scarce Swift *Schoutedenapus myoptilus*

Booted Eagle *Hieraaetus pennatus*

Forktailed Drongo *Dicrurus adsimilis*

Helmeted Guineafowl *Numida meleagris*

Indian Myna *Acridotheres tristis*

Spurwinged Goose *Plectropterus gambensis*

Burntnecked Eremomela *Eremomela usticollis*

Cape Sugarbird *Promerops cafer*

Black Eagle *Aquila verreauxii*

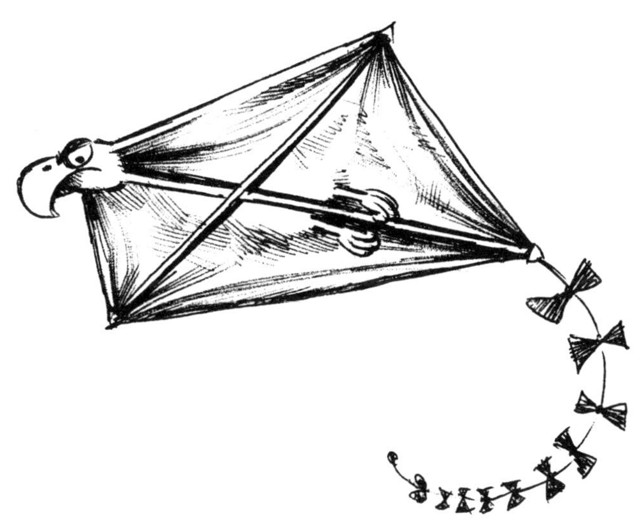

Yellowbilled Kite *Milvus migrans*

Gabar Goshawk *Micronisus gabar*

Fairy Flycatcher *Stenostira scita*

Hooded Vulture *Necrosyrtes monachus*

Bronze Mannikin *Spermestes cucullatus*

Lazy Cisticola *Cisticola aberrans*

Bat Hawk *Macheiramphus alcinus*

African Black Oystercatcher *Haematopus moquini*

Martial Eagle *Polemaetus bellicosus*

Secretarybird *Sagittarius serpentarius*, making a
Sandwich Tern *Sterna sandvicensis*

Stone(d)chat *Saxicola torquata*

Jameson's Firefinch **(extinguished version)** *Lagonosticta rhodopareia*

Knot *Calidris canutus*

African Fish Eagle *Haliaeetus vocifer*

Laughing Dove *Streptopelia senegalensis*

Macaroni Penguin *Eudyptes chrysolophus*

Blackeyed Bulbul *Pycnonotus barbatus*

Cinderella Waxbill *Estrilda thomensis*

Cuckoo Hawk *Aviceda cuculoides*

Bully Canary *Serinus sulphuratus*

Pied Kingfisher *Ceryle rudis*

Wailing Cisticola *Cisticola lais*

Hamerkop *Scopus umbretta*

Blacksmith Plover *Vanellus armatus*

Cutthroat Finch *Amadina fasciata*

Lemonbreasted Canary *Serinus citrinipectus*

Bearded Robin *Erythropygia quadrivirgata*